CAREER EXPLORATION

Police Detective

by Tracey Boraas

Consultant:
Roseann Campagnoli
Public Information Officer
Hennepin County Sheriff's Office
Minneapolis, Minnesota

CAPSTONE BOOKS
an imprint of Capstone Press
Mankato, Minnesota

Capstone Books are published by Capstone Press
151 Good Counsel Drive, P.O. Box 669, Mankato, Minnesota 56002
http://www.capstone-press.com

Printed in the United States of America.

Library of Congress Cataloging-in-Publication Data
Boraas, Tracey.
Police Detective/by Tracey Boraas.
p. cm.—(Career exploration)
Includes bibliographical references and index.
Summary: Introduces the career of police detective, focusing on educational requirements, duties, workplace, salary, employment outlook, and possible future positions.
ISBN 0-7368-0597-4
1. Detectives—Juvenile literature. 2. Criminal investigation—Juvenile literature. [1. Detectives. 2. Criminal investigation—Vocational guidance. 3. Vocational guidance.] I. Title. II. Series.
HV7922 .B65 2001
363.25'023'73—dc21 00-021541

Editorial Credits
Leah K. Pockrandt, editor; Steve Christensen, cover designer; Kia Bielke, production designer and illustrator; Heidi Schoof and Kimberly Danger, photo researchers

Photo Credits
David F. Clobes, cover, 8, 11, 12, 15, 16, 23, 30, 36, 40, 42
Index Stock Imagery/Gary A. Conner, 20
International Stock/Phyllis Picardi, 26; George Ancona, 29
Unicorn Stock Photos/Robin Rudd, 6; A. Ramey, 19, 39; Dennis MacDonald, 33

Special thanks to the Hennepin County Sheriff's Office, Investigative Division, Uniformed Patrol Division, K-9 Unit for their assistance with this book.

1 2 3 4 5 6 06 05 04 03 02 01

Table of Contents

Fast Facts

Career Title	Police Detective
O*NET Number	63011A
DOT Cluster (Dictionary of Occupational Titles)	Service occupations
DOT Number	375.267-010
GOE Number (Guide for Occupational Exploration)	04.01.02
NOC Number (National Occupational Classification-Canada)	626
Salary Range (U.S. Bureau of Labor Statistics, Human Resources Development Canada, and other industry sources, late 1990s figures)	U.S.: $19,200 to $64,500 Canada: $27,300 to $71,960 (Canadian dollars)
Minimum Educational Requirements	U.S.: associate's or bachelor's degree Canada: diploma or bachelor's degree
Certification/Licensing Requirements	U.S.: required Canada: required

Subject Knowledge	Public safety and security; law; government; clerical; psychology; sociology and anthropology; geography, foreign language; computer science; public relations; public speaking
Personal Abilities/Skills	Work with laws and regulations, sometimes written in legal language; use practical thinking to conduct or supervise investigations; supervise other workers; plan the work of a department or activity; deal with various kinds of people; work under pressure or in dangerous situations; keep physically fit; use guns and other safety devices
Job Outlook	U.S.: average growth Canada: good
Personal Interests	Protective: interest in the use of authority to protect people and property
Similar Types of Jobs	Police officer; constable; correction officer; guard; bailiff; sheriff or deputy sheriff; special agent

Chapter 1

Police Detective

Police detectives protect people and property. They carry out investigations to solve criminal cases. They search for clues and interview people to determine the facts. Detectives also are called criminal investigators. Some Canadian law enforcement agencies do not use the term detective. But many Canadian law enforcement officers perform the duties of detectives.

Police detectives are plainclothes police officers. They wear suits, jackets, and pants instead of uniforms. This helps them blend in with the public as they investigate crimes.

Police Detectives' Duties

Police detectives conduct investigations to solve crimes. Detectives usually are assigned to specific types of cases. For example, some detectives

Plainclothes police detectives conduct investigations to solve crimes.

Police detectives sometimes conduct surveillance.

investigate illegal drug cases. Others work to solve murder cases.

Information that helps police detectives solve crimes is called evidence. Detectives gather evidence in a variety of ways. They search for clues at crime scenes. They interview victims, witnesses, and suspects. Suspects are people who may be guilty of crimes.

Detectives may perform surveillance during investigations. They watch certain businesses or homes to gain information about suspects or crimes. Detectives often observe and photograph illegal activities during surveillance. They arrest suspects when the evidence proves that suspects were involved in the crimes.

Police detectives may schedule polygraph tests for suspects and witnesses. Polygraph tests also are called lie detector tests. These tests measure people's body reactions as they answer questions. The test results can indicate the truthfulness of witnesses or suspects. But polygraph tests usually cannot be used as evidence in court.

Police detectives maintain a file on each case they investigate. Detectives record interview information and list the evidence they found. They also record the results of polygraph tests and other facts related to the investigation.

Police detectives prepare cases for court. Prosecuting attorneys use the information and evidence detectives gathered. During trials, these lawyers try to convince a jury or judge that a suspect is guilty. These lawyers work for local, state, provincial, or federal governments. Detectives testify in court about the information they have gathered.

Equipment

Police detectives use several pieces of equipment. They carry a badge and other identification. These items show that they work for a particular law enforcement department or agency. Detectives carry firearms. Detectives keep firearms close to their bodies in secure holders called holsters. Detectives use firearms to protect themselves and other people from criminals. Detectives also carry handcuffs.

Police detectives use several pieces of communication equipment. They use two-way radios. Some of these radios are mounted in detectives' cars. Detectives also carry smaller two-way radios. They use these radios to send and receive messages from the police station. This station often is called headquarters. Detectives also may carry cellular phones or pagers. Detectives use these devices to communicate when they are away from their cars.

Detectives drive unmarked cars. These cars do not look like most police cars. They do not have police lights or the police unit's name painted on their doors. Detectives can work undercover or conduct surveillance without suspects recognizing

Police detectives often use cellular phones on the job.

their cars. But unmarked police cars still contain standard police equipment such as two-way radios.

Police detectives also use computers. They search police databases for information. These computer files organize and store information. Detectives write reports about the evidence that they gather. They create files to record their own activities throughout the investigation. Photos also can be scanned and stored in computer files. Police detectives can show these photos to witnesses to help them identify suspects.

SHERIFF

Chapter 2

Day-to-Day Activities

Police detectives' duties vary each day. Detectives work by themselves and with partners. These detectives share duties on criminal cases. Detectives perform some duties at their offices and other duties in the community.

Headquarters

Police detectives usually begin each day in their offices. They review current cases and look over new cases assigned by their commanding officers. They use computers to search police databases and look for information to help solve cases.

Police detectives also use computers to retrieve information from federal agencies. For example, they use Federal Bureau of Investigation (FBI)

Police detectives often begin their day by reviewing current cases.

files to try to match fingerprints from crime scenes. Detectives sometimes cannot match fingerprints with those in their department files. FBI files include the fingerprints of millions of people.

Detectives do additional work at headquarters after they investigate cases. Detectives send any physical evidence to crime labs. This evidence may include bullets, clothing, or hair. At crime labs, crime lab technicians test the evidence. Technicians may find blood, hair, bits of skin, or cloth fibers. Technicians try to prove if these pieces of evidence came from suspects or victims. Detectives receive reports on the evidence tests.

Police detectives may question witnesses or suspects at headquarters. They often record their interviews on audio or videotape. These records can be useful if detectives have to testify in court.

Some detectives work with ballistics experts. These people are experts on firearms and bullets. Ballistics experts may use computers to match weapons and bullets found at crime scenes.

Detectives write down details about every piece of evidence they find during their investigations. They may make prints of shoeprints or note the location of discharged bullets. But crime scene

Police detectives use computers to review FBI files.

technicians perform these duties in large law enforcement agencies. In Canada, these technicians are called forensic identification specialists.

Police detectives put together everything they learn about their cases into files. They study the information. They then write case reports.

In the Community

Police detectives also perform much of their work in the community. They follow up on crime scene clues. They may visit a suspect's workplace or

Police detectives arrest suspects after they have gathered enough evidence.

home. Detectives talk to people who can give them information about the suspect's behavior.

Detectives sometimes get tips about crimes that are being planned. They may work undercover to learn about these plans. Undercover detectives do not identify themselves as police officers. They sometimes pose as criminals. These actions can help them obtain information they could not otherwise find. Detectives also conduct surveillance from their cars or other locations.

After gathering information, detectives may have enough information to arrest suspects. They call for back-up support from other police officers. They obtain warrants. These documents allow law enforcement officials to search buildings for evidence. Detectives then may arrest the suspects.

Specialty Areas

Detectives in large law enforcement agencies usually specialize in investigating certain types of cases. They specialize in one of three main categories of investigative work. These areas are crimes against persons, crimes against property, and proactive cases.

Police detectives in small communities may not have as many crimes to investigate. These detectives then perform other routine police officer duties. For example, they may patrol streets or respond to traffic accidents.

Crimes Against Persons

Law enforcement agencies usually consider crimes against persons to be the most important cases. This is because these types of crimes directly affect people. These crimes include murder, kidnapping, and sexual assault.

Police detectives at large law enforcement agencies may specialize in certain types of crimes against persons. For example, large cities have homicide detectives who investigate murders and some accidental deaths. These detectives are on call 24 hours a day. They often are called to work in the middle of the night. Many murders and accidents occur during that time.

Crimes Against Property

Police detectives who work on crimes against property investigate cases in which property was involved. These crimes may include burglary, theft, or arson. Arson involves using fire to destroy buildings and property.

Detectives often review crimes against property for patterns. Criminals who commit these crimes often repeat the same crime pattern. A common pattern among several crimes may lead the detective to the criminal.

Proactive Cases

Detectives in proactive cases investigate cases that occur on a regular basis over a period of time. These crimes include liquor violations,

Some police detectives specialize in investigating one type of crime such as proactive crime.

illegal gambling, the sale of illegal drugs, and gang violence.

Proactive cases can be difficult to solve. Detectives may work on these cases for several months. They sometimes work undercover.

Detectives assigned to proactive cases usually work evening shifts. Many of these crimes occur between 6 p.m. and 2 a.m.

Chapter 3

The Right Candidate

Police detectives need a variety of skills, interests, and personal qualities. They should be honest. They need to have good judgment and a strong sense of responsibility. Police detectives should enjoy working with people. They need good decision-making and social skills. They need to be able to work in dangerous situations.

Interests

Police detectives must be interested in protecting people and property. Detectives in North America take an oath when they enter the profession. Detectives make this formal promise to act with honesty and in the best interest of the public. The oath also includes a promise to uphold the laws of their country.

Police detectives need good communication skills.

Police detectives should enjoy mental challenges. Detectives must recognize anything unusual at crime scenes. They must be able to figure out what clues mean. They use deductive thinking to put the clues together like a puzzle.

Detectives should be interested in justice. They should enjoy helping people. They should feel a sense of accomplishment when their investigations lead to criminals' arrests or convictions.

Abilities and Skills

Police detectives must understand legal language. Detectives need to understand the laws and regulations they enforce. They must follow a variety of procedures and rules. These include local, state, provincial, or federal rules. Detectives must understand how these laws both protect them and limit their authority. Detectives also must understand victims' and suspects' rights.

Detectives must use logic to conduct investigations. They must be able to use clues and evidence to determine when and how a crime occurred.

Police detectives often work with a variety of people such as suspects and witnesses.

Police detectives must be able to work with a variety of people. They work with partners and other law enforcement personnel. They speak with attorneys. They interview crime victims. They inform victims' families when victims are injured or killed. Detectives need to be respectful to these people while performing their duties.

Detectives also must deal with suspects. These people may be disrespectful. They may lie to the

Skills

Workplace Skills

	Yes	No
Resources:		
Assign use of time	✓	☐
Assign use of money	☐	✓
Assign use of material and facility resources	✓	☐
Assign use of human resources	✓	☐
Interpersonal Skills:		
Take part as a member of a team	✓	☐
Teach others	✓	☐
Serve clients/customers	✓	☐
Show leadership	✓	☐
Work with others to arrive at a decision	✓	☐
Work with a variety of people	✓	☐
Information:		
Acquire and judge information	✓	☐
Understand and follow legal requirements	✓	☐
Organize and maintain information	✓	☐
Understand and communicate information	✓	☐
Use computers to process information	✓	☐
Systems:		
Identify, understand, and work with systems	✓	☐
Understand environmental, social, political, economic, or business systems	✓	☐
Oversee and correct system performance	☐	✓
Improve and create systems	☐	✓
Technology:		
Select technology	✓	☐
Apply technology to task	✓	☐
Maintain and troubleshoot technology	✓	☐

Foundation Skills

	Yes	No
Basic Skills:		
Read	✓	☐
Write	✓	☐
Do arithmetic and math	✓	☐
Speak and listen	✓	☐
Thinking Skills:		
Learn	✓	☐
Reason	✓	☐
Think creatively	✓	☐
Make decisions	✓	☐
Solve problems	✓	☐
Personal Qualities:		
Take individual responsibility	✓	☐
Have self-esteem and self-management	✓	☐
Be sociable	✓	☐
Be fair, honest, and sincere	✓	☐

police detectives. Suspects may verbally or physically threaten detectives. Detectives need to handle these suspects calmly. They need to be able to think through a situation and respond quickly and appropriately.

Police detectives must be alert and physically fit. They may need to defend themselves against attacks from criminals or suspects. They may have to chase suspects. Detectives sometimes need to physically control suspects during arrests.

Detectives must be able to work in stressful situations. They frequently handle conflicts between people. They often deal with unpleasant or angry people. They work under the constant threat of danger. Detectives have a higher injury rate than people in many other jobs.

Detectives must be able to work in physically unpleasant environments. They may conduct their investigations in dark, abandoned buildings. They may work in rain, heat, or cold as they search outdoor areas for clues.

POLIC

Chapter 4

Preparing for the Career

Most police detectives begin their careers as licensed peace officers. In Canada, these officers are called constables. Police officers work for local law enforcement departments. Deputies work for county sheriffs' offices.

In Canada, some detectives work for city police departments. Others work for the Royal Canadian Mounted Police (RCMP). This is Canada's national police force. The RCMP also is the police force in every province and territory except Ontario, Quebec, and parts of Newfoundland.

High School Education

High school students interested in becoming police detectives should study a variety of

Most detectives begin their careers as peace officers.

subjects. Students learn verbal and written communication skills in speech and English classes. Foreign language studies also are helpful. Detectives often deal with people who speak languages other than English. Students learn about history, civics, and government in social studies classes. Students also may learn about victims' and suspects' rights in these classes.

Computer classes may benefit students who want to become police detectives. Detectives use computers to write reports and retrieve information from databases. Many criminals also use computers to commit crimes such as fraud. These criminals may try to steal money from other people's bank accounts or use other people's credit cards. Computer knowledge may help police detectives arrest these criminals.

Students also benefit from physical education courses and sports. Detectives need to be in good physical shape. They sometimes chase suspects for long distances. They also may need to restrain suspects and defend themselves against attacks.

Requirements

Police detectives are government employees. In the United States, these jobs are filled through

Sports activities are beneficial to high school students who want to be police detectives.

a formal testing process. Candidates are rated according to their test scores. Law enforcement agencies may use this list when hiring.

Detectives also must hold a valid peace officers' license in their state. License requirements vary depending on the state.

Police detectives first must meet police officer requirements. All police officer candidates must pass a background check. Police departments investigate candidates to find if they ever have

Police detectives must know how to safely fire a gun.

been arrested or convicted of crimes. People who have been convicted of serious crimes such as domestic assault cannot be police officers.

Police officer candidates also must meet local civil service regulations. Candidates usually must be at least 21 years old. They must meet certain height and weight standards. They must pass written and physical exams. Police officer candidates must successfully complete an interview and personality test. They must have a valid driver's license. They often must pass a drug screening test.

All states have some standards for police officers. The Police Officers Standards and Training Commission (POST Board) is an agency that sets standards for police officer training programs. California created the first POST Board in 1959. Today, each U.S. state has an agency similar to the POST Board.

Experienced police officers can apply for detective jobs. Each law enforcement agency has its own requirements for promotion to detective positions. Some agencies promote officers to detective positions based on experience and job performance. Other agencies require officers to complete post-secondary education programs.

Post-Secondary Education

Police officers' educational requirements vary. Most departments require officers to have a high school education. Most departments also require officers to have some post-secondary education.

People interested in becoming police officers can attend police academies, technical schools, community colleges, or universities. People earn an associate's degree by completing a program of study at a technical school or college. In Canada, people earn a diploma from a community college. Students usually earn a diploma or associate's degree in two years.

Some police detectives earn a bachelor's degree in law enforcement or criminal justice. People earn this degree by completing a course of study at a college or university. People usually earn this degree in about four years. Some police detectives have a master's degree. Students earn this degree by completing an advanced course of study at a college or university. Most people complete this degree in about two years.

In Canada, many people attend the RCMP training academy. The minimum educational requirement is a high school diploma. But many candidates have completed some post-secondary education. Some candidates have a college diploma or certificate. But others have a bachelor's degree or master's degree.

In the United States, police academy courses meet standards set by state agencies such as the POST Board. Law enforcement experts usually conduct this training. Police academy training programs can last from three to nine months.

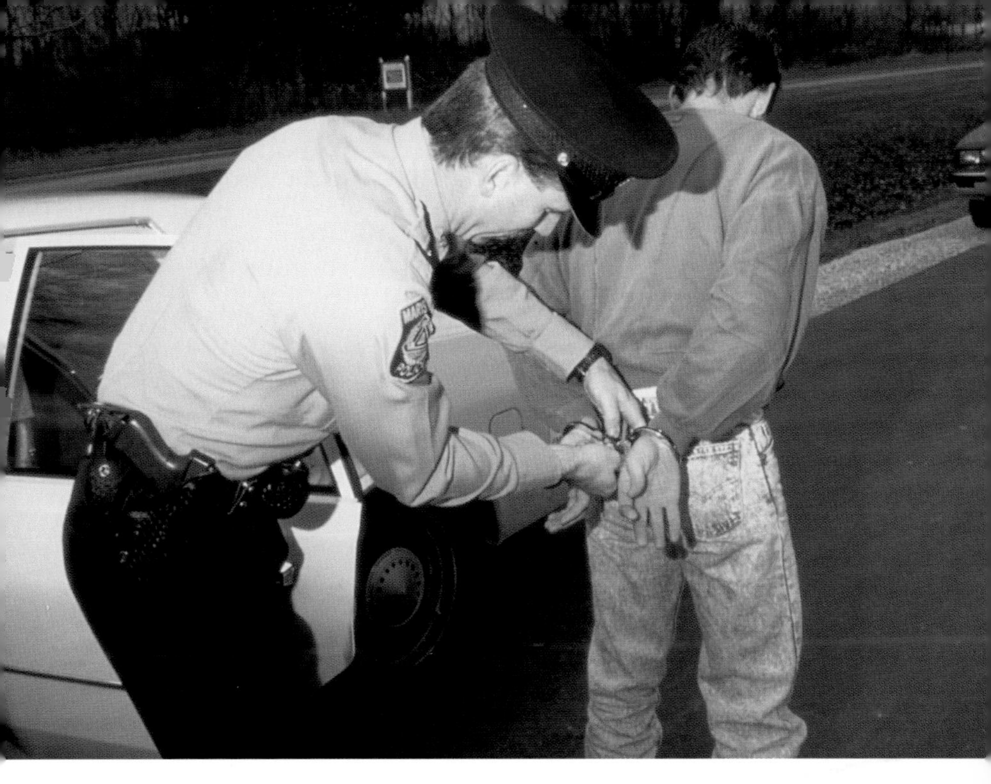

Police officers must know how to restrain suspects.

Police officer candidates study a variety of topics. They take classes on constitutional law and civil rights. They study state and local laws. Candidates learn how to investigate accidents. They learn how to patrol, control traffic, and do pursuit driving. They learn to safely pursue suspects in cars. Candidates learn how to use handcuffs to restrain suspects. They also learn to defend themselves with self-defense techniques and weapons such as guns and batons.

High School Diploma → Post-Secondary Education → Field Training

Some state governments also may offer training programs. Large agencies such as the FBI or groups of regional agencies may offer these programs.

Field Training

New police officers must complete between 220 and 550 hours of field training. In Canada, new RCMP officers must complete six months of field training. During this training, new police officers work with experienced police officers in actual situations. The experienced officers supervise and evaluate the new police officers.

During field training, new police officers apply skills such as pursuit driving and danger recognition. They try to control suspects without unnecessary injury or force. They also learn when and when not to use weapons.

Civil Service Requirements (United States)

Licensing

Continuing Education

Continuing Education

In the United States, all law enforcement professionals need to continue their education to maintain their licenses. Detectives are required to take a specific number of course hours each year. State training agencies, police academies, and large law enforcement agencies often offer these courses on site. These in-service training sessions usually last from one day to two weeks.

Police officers who want to become detectives can take classes that focus on investigative techniques. These courses may help officers develop special skills or prepare them for career advancement. Some courses focus on topics such as new technology or management skills.

INTELLIGENCE
ARREST BULLETIN
RE-ISSUE ARREST BULL

Chapter 5

The Market

The job market for police detectives is favorable in most areas of North America. Police detectives' job opportunities may vary with location and level of education.

Salary

Police detective jobs are government jobs. These jobs have set salary ranges. Local governments set these salary ranges. The salaries are based on education and experience requirements. Community size and location also affect the government salary scale.

In the United States, police detectives earn between $19,200 and $58,500 per year. Detectives with supervisory duties earn between $22,500 and $64,500 per year. In

Job opportunities are good for police detectives in most areas of North America.

Canada, police detectives earn between $27,300 and $71,960 per year.

Benefits

Police detectives usually receive benefits in addition to their salaries. These benefits include paid vacation and sick leave. They also may include medical and life insurance.

Detectives usually can retire with a pension after 20 or 25 years of service. A pension is an amount of money paid regularly to a retired person. Detectives' pensions may be equal to half of their salary at retirement.

Job Outlook

In the United States, the job market for detectives is expected to have average growth. Job openings usually occur when detectives change occupations or retire.

The number of police detective jobs can vary from year to year. Local governments study their communities' law enforcement

Job opportunities are based on local, state, provincial, or federal law enforcement needs.

needs. They decide how much will be spent on law enforcement jobs.

In Canada, the job market for police detectives is good. Cutbacks by the government in law enforcement jobs may reduce detective positions. But most law enforcement positions are needed to maintain public safety.

Some police detectives advance to management positions such as detective supervisors.

The job market for police detectives can be competitive. Law enforcement is becoming more scientific. People who have studied police science, computer science, or criminal justice have the best opportunities.

Advancement

Most police detectives advance in one of two ways. Some advance through specialized investigative areas such as crimes against people. Others advance into management positions. Experienced detectives may become supervisors. In the United States, supervisors then may advance to positions such as captains, chiefs of police, or police commissioners. In Canada, experienced detectives may advance to positions such as inspectors, superintendents, or commissioners. Each advancement level may require additional education.

Police detectives with additional training may have more advancement opportunities. Detectives can take continuing education courses to improve their investigative skills.

Related Careers

Many career opportunities exist for people interested in law enforcement. They may become police officers or constables, sheriffs and deputy sheriffs, state patrol officers, or U.S. marshals. State patrol officers work for state governments.

SHERIFF

These officers also are called state troopers or highway patrol officers. Marshals work for the U.S. Marshals Service.

Some people interested in law enforcement become special agents. These people work for federal agencies. These agencies include the Internal Revenue Service or the Bureau of Alcohol, Tobacco, and Firearms. Federal agents enforce laws specific to their agencies.

People interested in security and helping others have many other job opportunities. They can become guards, bailiffs, or correctional officers. Bailiffs work at courthouses. They swear in witnesses and perform other courtroom duties. Correctional officers maintain security in prisons.

Public safety will continue to be an important issue in the future. People want to live and work in safe communities. Police detectives and other law enforcement officers will be needed to solve crimes and keep communities safe.

Police detectives will continue to be needed to keep communities safe.

Words to Know

ballistics (buh-LISS-tiks)—the science and study of bullets that are fired from guns

case (KAYSS)—a crime that police detectives investigate

conviction (kuhn-VIK-shuhn)—a judgment of guilt against a suspect

evidence (EV-uh-duhnss)—information, items, and facts that help prove something is true or false

investigation (in-vess-tuh-GAY-shuhn)—the act of searching for facts to solve a crime

suspect (SUHSS-pekt)—a person believed to be responsible for a crime

victim (VIK-tuhm)—a person who is hurt, killed, or made to suffer because of an accident or crime

witness (WIT-niss)—a person who has seen or heard something about a crime or accident

To Learn More

Camenson, Blythe. *Careers for Legal Eagles and Other Law-and-Order Types.* VGM Careers for You. Lincolnwood, Ill.: VGM Career Horizons, 1998.

Camenson, Blythe. *Careers for Mystery Buffs and Other Snoops and Sleuths.* VGM Careers for You. Lincolnwood, Ill.: VGM Career Horizons, 1997.

Cosgrove, Holli, ed. *Career Discovery Encyclopedia.* Vol. 3. 4th ed. Chicago: Ferguson Publishing, 2000.

Goldberg, Jan. *Careers for Courageous People and Other Adventurous Types.* VGM Careers for You. Lincolnwood, Ill.: VGM Career Horizons, 1998.

Stinchcomb, James D. *Opportunities in Law Enforcement and Criminal Justice Careers.* VGM Opportunities. Lincolnwood, Ill.: VGM Career Horizons, 1996.

Useful Addresses

Canadian Police Association
100-141 rue Catherine St.
Ottawa, ON K2P 1C3
Canada

International Union of Police Associations
1421 Prince Street
Suite 330
Alexandria, VA 22314

Police Foundation
1201 Connecticut Avenue NW
Suite 200
Washington, DC 20036

Royal Canadian Mounted Police
100 Vanier Parkway
Ottawa, ON K1A 0R2
Canada

Internet Sites

Crime Scene Investigation
http://police2.ucr.edu/csi.html

Job Futures—Police Officers and Firefighters
http://www.hrdc-drhc.gc.ca/corp/stratpol/arb/jobs/english/volume1/626/626.htm

Occupational Outlook Handbook — Police and Detectives
http://stats.bls.gov/oco/ocos160.htm

The Police Station
http://www.wwlia.org/police.htm

Royal Canadian Mounted Police
http://www.rcmp-grc.gc.ca/frames/rcmp-grc1.htm

Index